# MEX TRAVEL GUIDE

## 2023

### The Ultimate And Updated Travel Guide To Explore Mexico In 2023, Everything You Need To Know

**Kevin M. Staples**

**Copyright © 2023 by Kevin M. Staples**

All rights reserved. No part of this publication may be reproduced, distributed, or transmitted in any form or by any means, including photocopying, recording, or other electronic or mechanical methods, without the prior written permission of the publisher, except in the case of brief quotations embodied in critical reviews and certain other noncommercial uses permitted by copyright law. For permission requests, write to the publisher at the address below.

*Mexico travel guide 2023*

# Table Of Contents

INTRODUCTION TO MEXICO..............................5

Overview Of Mexico............................. 8

CHAPTER ONE....................... 11

Interesting Facts About Mexico........................ 11

History Of Mexico............................15

Geography Of Mexico..........................18

Climate Of Mexico.................... 21

Culture Of Mexico....................24

CHAPTER TWO......................29

Visa Requirements To Visit Mexico....................29

Important things To Know Before Visiting Mexico...................... 32

Best Time To Visit Mexico For The Best Experience..........................36

Basic Spanish Phrases To Interact With The Locals....................40

Things To Bring Along On Your Trip To Mexico... 44

CHAPTER THREE.................................49

Getting Around Mexico........................ 49

Practical Steps To Stay Safe In Mexico...............53

Do's And Don'ts In Mexico............................... 57

CHAPTER FOUR...................... 62

Interesting Things To Do In Mexico...................62

Historical Sites To See In Mexico........................ 66

Top Museums And Galleries In Mexico.............70

Parks And Gardens In Mexico............................ 73
CHAPTER FIVE........................................ 78
Shopping In Mexico.................................. 78
Events And Festivals In Mexico.....................81
Nightlife In Mexico..................................85
CHAPTER SIX......................................89
Budget Friendly Hotels In Mexico....................89
Mid-range Hotels In Mexico........................ 92
Luxury Hotels In Mexico...........................95
Camping In Mexico.................................98
CHAPTER SEVEN................................. 102
Budget Friendly Restaurants In Mexico........... 102
Mid-range Restaurants In Mexico...................104
Luxury Restaurants In Mexico..................... 107
Cafes And Coffee Shops In Mexico.................111
CHAPTER EIGHT..................................115
Spanish Cuisines To Try.......................... 115
International Cuisines To Try...................... 118
CHAPTER NINE...................................123
10 - Days Itinerary To Explore Mexico............. 123
CONCLUSION...................................... 127

# INTRODUCTION TO MEXICO

Thomas set off on a trip to Mexico, a country with a lively culture and a long history since he was an inquisitive and daring traveler. He entered this magical nation for the very first time with open arms and wide eyes.

Thomas was enthralled by Mexico City's bustling streets the instant he arrived. Street food's delicious scent permeated the air as busy roads were bordered by vibrant buildings covered in elaborate paintings. His desire to discover more was piqued by the city's pulsating Mariachi music.

Thomas went to the Teotihuacan ruins, eager to learn more about the native way of life. He was in awe of the ancient civilization's magnificent architectural design as he stood in front of the enormous pyramids. He was filled with wonder and respect as he ascended the Pyramid of the

Sun because of the history that was happening beneath him.

Thomas continued on his adventure and arrived at the enchanted city of Oaxaca. He spent time there steeped in the colorful customs of the Day of the Dead celebration. He participated in the merry processions, commemorating the deceased with marigold and sugar skull offerings while wearing a mask painted with a skull. Thomas felt a strong connection to the Mexican people and their respect for life and death as the streets came alive with exuberant celebration.

Thomas came to the magnificent beaches of Tulum in search of serenity in the natural world. He was enveloped by crystal-clear waves and immaculate white dunes as he took in the sun's warmth. He investigated the mysterious cenotes, which the ancient Mayans considered to be holy natural sinkholes. As he dove into the glistening waters, he experienced calm and renewal.

Thomas experienced warmth and generosity at every step as he traveled across Mexico. People in the area welcomed him with sincere grins and told him about their lives, giving him a look into how they lived. Thomas seized every chance to immerse himself in the vivid tapestry of Mexican culture, from eating delectable tacos to learning traditional dances.

Thomas said goodbye to Mexico with a sorrowful heart, having been transformed by his wonderful adventures. He had developed a strong awareness of the world's variety and a drive for adventure as a result of the country. He knew that Mexico will always have a particular place in his heart, so when he boarded the aircraft, he brought with him the memories, the colors, the tastes, and the energy of that country.

Thus, Thomas's first trip to Mexico turned into a life-changing voyage of discovery that left a lasting impression on his spirit and motivated him to set out on subsequent journeys with a hunger for exploration and an appreciation of the beauty that exists outside of his own country.

# Overview Of Mexico

Welcome to Mexico, a place renowned for its vivid colors, rich past, and many cultures. This travel guide will provide you with the essential information, unknown sites, and insider tips you need to make the most of your trip while guiding you in exploring this fascinating country's charms.

Mexico is a country that expertly blends ancient traditions with modern allure. Whether amid the enigmatic ruins of Chichen Itza or the hectic streets of Mexico City, every step reveals a narrative just waiting to be discovered. No matter what their hobbies are, whether they are serious history buffs, nature lovers, foodies, or simply want to relax on sun-kissed beaches, every visitor can find something to stimulate their interest in Mexico.

Immerse yourself in the vibrant culture of Mexico, where colorful fiestas erupt on the streets, mariachi music fills the air, and exquisite folk art adorns the markets. Explore the stunning architecture of old colonial cities like Guanajuato and Oaxaca, whose meandering cobblestone streets and ornate facades transport you to another era.

Discover the amazing natural wonders that make up the diverse geography of Mexico. Discover the enigmatic cenotes of the Yucatan Peninsula, which are underwater sinkholes with pleasant green waters that call you to swim in them. Set off on a hike through the Copper Canyon, an impressive network of gorges that rivals the magnificence of the Grand Canyon.

Take pleasure in the delectable flavor of Mexican cuisine, which mixes indigenous ingredients with Spanish influences. Every cuisine in the country, from the spiciest salsas to the aromatic mole sauces, represents the history of its culinary culture. Eat fresh seafood by the sea, indulge in authentic street cuisine, and savor flavorful traditional dishes like tamales and enchiladas.

Prepare to be amazed by the gorgeous beaches of Mexico along the Riviera Maya, where exquisite white sands and the turquoise waters of the Caribbean Sea combine. Dive into the second-largest coral reef system in the world, the Mesoamerican Barrier Reef, which is home to a variety of vibrant marine life and spectacular coral formations.

This book will guide you through each area of Mexico, giving you important details on the must-see attractions, hidden gems, accessible modes of transportation, and local customs. Let this book be your travel companion as you go on an extraordinary voyage through a country that will warmly welcome you and make a lasting effect on your soul, whether you are a regular visitor to Mexico or a first-time visitor. Prepare to create lifetime memories amid Mexico's stunning tapestry.

# CHAPTER ONE

## *Interesting Facts About Mexico*

Mexico is a country with a fascinating history, enduring cultural customs, and breathtaking natural beauty. The most intriguing characteristics that make Mexico such a fantastic tourism destination are listed here.

- Ancient Civilizations: Among the illustrious prehistoric civilizations that once thrived in Mexico were the Maya, Aztec, and Olmec. Their great structures, including the dominating Teotihuacan pyramids and the unmistakable Chichen Itza, are proof of their in-depth knowledge and cultural prowess.

- Mexico has an incredible 35 locations that have been named UNESCO World Heritage Sites. These destinations, which include the magnificent historic center of Mexico City, Palenque, and the pre-Hispanic city of Monte Albán, illustrate Mexico's extensive history and extraordinary value on a global scale.

- Day of the Dead: The Day of the Dead, sometimes referred to as Dia de los Muertos, is a two-day holiday held in Mexico on November 1 and 2. This vibrant and colorful holiday honors departed loved ones with elaborate altars, sugar skulls, marigold flowers, and lively processions. It is a very unique mix of indigenous and Catholic traditions.

- Mexican cuisine is renowned for its robust flavor and wide range of ingredients. The delectable fusion of indigenous and European influences can be found in everything from tacos and tamales to guacamole and mole in the culinary delights of Mexico. Even Mexican cuisine has been acknowledged by UNESCO as an Intangible Cultural Heritage of Humanity.

- Biodiversity: Mexico is considered one of the world's megadiverse countries due to its astounding range of plant and animal species. It is home to around 10-12% of the world's biodiversity and has a variety of ecosystems, including deserts, mangroves, and coral reefs in addition to tropical rainforests and rainforests.

- Mariachi music is a well-known example of Mexican culture and is distinguished by its vibrant rhythms and passionate melodies. It comes from the state of Jalisco and features traditional instruments including the guitar, trumpet, violin, and vihuela. Mariachi bands may be heard performing at celebrations and weddings all across the country.

- Cenotes: The Yucatan Peninsula in Mexico is home to interesting cenotes, which are natural sinkholes formed by collapsing limestone. Swimming, snorkeling, and diving in these crystal-clear underground pools may reveal a hidden world of underwater tunnels and strange geological features.

- Mesoamerican Ballgame: A game called "ulama," which originated in Mesoamerica, was played by the Maya and Aztec. It was a significant cultural and religious event that used rubber balls and stone courts. The game's rules constantly altered, but they always included a struggle between the forces of light and evil.

- Tequila and Mezcal: Two of Mexico's most well-known distilled beverages are tequila and mezcal. The majority of tequila, which is made by distilling blue agave, is manufactured in Jalisco. Mezcal, on the other hand, is prepared from a variety of agave species and is associated with Oaxaca. These beverages have gained international recognition due to their unique flavors and cultural significance.

Each year, an incredible migration path takes millions of monarch butterflies from Canada and the United States to Michoacán state in Mexico. One of the most astounding natural phenomena in the world, these small mammals travel hundreds of kilometers to seek sanctuary in the oyamel fir forests of Mexico.

## History Of Mexico

With a history spanning thousands of years, Mexico is a nation rich in culture and history. The Olmecs, who existed circa 1200 BC in the Gulf of Mexico, were the first known civilizations in Mexico. The Mayans, who thrived in the Yucatan Peninsula and its environs from around 2000 BC to 1500 AD, were their successors. The Mayans achieved tremendous advancements in astronomy, mathematics, and construction in addition to constructing beautiful cities and creating a written language.

The Aztecs became the main force in central Mexico in the fourteenth century. They built

Tenochtitlan, their capital city, on an island in the center of Lake Texcoco, and used commerce and conquest to expand their huge empire. The Aztecs also produced significant improvements in agriculture, health, and engineering, as well as in culture and science.

Hernan Cortes, a Spanish conqueror, landed in Mexico in 1519 intending to seize its riches and territory for the Spanish Crown. Tenochtitlan was taken by Cortes in 1521, essentially ending Aztec dominion in Mexico after a series of conflicts and alliances with local peoples. The local population was subjected to the Spanish colonial government's linguistic, religious, and cultural encroachments.

After a protracted and brutal conflict led by individuals like Miguel Hidalgo and Jose Maria Morelos, Mexico finally achieved independence from Spain in 1821. Foreign interference, economic inequality, and political corruption were continuous problems for the newly independent nation as it worked to build stability. The Mexican Revolution began in 1910, with diverse groups vying for political control, worker rights, and land reform. In the end, the revolution brought forth a new constitution in 1917 as well as a period of political and social transformation.

Mexico went through phases of political stability and economic expansion in the decades that followed, as well as instability and armed conflict. Significant literary works by Octavio Paz and Carlos Fuentes, as well as the muralist movements of Diego Rivera, took place in the nation. Mexico has recently struggled with issues including drug trafficking, corruption, and immigration while also working to advance economic growth, human rights, and environmental sustainability.

The accomplishments and tribulations of its many ethnic groups and cultural traditions are reflected in Mexico's varied and variegated history. Mexico's history is a rich tapestry of human experience and accomplishment, spanning from the ancient civilizations of the Olmecs and Mayans to the colonial legacy of the Spanish, the revolution of the early 20th century, and the continuing problems and possibilities of the contemporary period.

## Geography Of Mexico

Mexico, which is a nation in southern North America, has a variety and breathtaking landscapes. Mexico's landscapes display the beauty and diversity that make it such an alluring destination, from imposing mountains to lush rainforests, vast deserts to stunning coasts.

Mexico, which stretches 1,900 miles from north to south, is bordered to the north by the United States and to the south by Guatemala and Belize. The nation is separated into a number of diverse areas, each with its own special geographical characteristics.

The Baja California Peninsula divides the Pacific Ocean from the Gulf of California along Mexico's northwest coast. This desert area is known for its stunning cliffs, rough mountains, and immaculate beaches, which make it a well-liked vacation spot for those who like the outdoors and water sports.

The Sierra Madre Occidental and Sierra Madre Oriental mountain ranges cut across the nation from west to east. In addition to providing beautiful views and fantastic chances for hiking, climbing, and animal viewing, these spectacular mountain ranges are renowned for their towering peaks, deep valleys, and thick forests.

The Yucatan Peninsula is located in southern Mexico and is the location of the world-famous Riviera Maya as well as the prehistoric Mayan ruins of Chichen Itza and Tulum. This area is a sanctuary for beach lovers and scuba diving aficionados because of its gorgeous turquoise seas, white sandy beaches, and complicated subterranean river systems known as cenotes.

The Mexican Plateau, commonly referred to as the Central Highlands, is found as you go farther south. This area is made up of broad plains and lush valleys that are sprinkled with quaint colonial villages and thriving metropolia like Mexico City, the nation's capital. The

Central Highlands, whose volcanic peaks like Popocatepetl and Iztaccihuatl dominate the skyline, provide a unique combination of cultural diversity and scenic splendor.

The lush jungles of the Chiapas Highlands replace the tropical rainforests of the Yucatan Peninsula to the southeast. Along with gushing waterfalls, thriving indigenous settlements, and the spectacular Palenque archaeological site, this area is home to a number of other natural attractions.

The immense Chihuahuan Desert, one of the biggest desert areas in North America, is also found in Mexico. This vast, dry desert region, which spans many northern Mexican states, is home to unusual plants and animals that have evolved to live in the desert's severe conditions.

In addition to creating breathtaking natural vistas, Mexico's diversified terrain also contributes to its abundant wildlife. The nation is a refuge for lovers of nature and animals since it is home to a diverse range of plant and animal species.

Mexico's terrain, which ranges from rough mountains to lush rainforests, is as varied as its history and culture. Every tourist may find something to enjoy when exploring the many landscapes of this amazing nation, whether they are looking for adventure, leisure, or cultural immersion.

## Climate Of Mexico

As varied as its topography, Mexico's climate offers a broad variety of climatic conditions across the nation. The diverse climatic zones present in Mexico are a result of changes in height, closeness to water bodies, and topographical factors.

Mexico's climate may be broadly classified into three types: tropical, moderate, and dry. The lowland regions near the beaches and in the southern part of the nation have a tropical climate. High temperatures and humidity are year-round characteristics of this zone, with very minor seasonal temperature variations. The tropical zone has average yearly temperatures between 25 and 28 degrees Celsius (77 and 82 degrees Fahrenheit). Sea breezes have an impact on coastal areas, helping to lower temperatures and provide cooling respite.

The central highland regions of Mexico, including Mexico City, have a temperate climate. In comparison to lowland areas, this region's height, which ranges from 1,800 to 2,400 meters (5,900 to 7,900 feet), results in colder temperatures. The temperate zone's yearly average temperature varies from 54 to 68 degrees Fahrenheit (12 to 20 degrees Celsius). There are two separate seasons—wet and dry—with the rainy one lasting from May to October. Winters may be chilly, with high-altitude temperatures hovering around the freezing mark.

The Sonoran Desert and the Baja California Peninsula are located in Mexico's northern and northwest, where there is an arid environment. Low rainfall and high temperatures are common in these regions, particularly in the summer. In the dry zone, summer temperatures often approach 40 degrees Celsius (104 degrees Fahrenheit), with an average yearly temperature in the range of 20 to 25 degrees Celsius (68 to 77 degrees Fahrenheit). The winters are warmer, with average highs of 50 to 68 degrees Fahrenheit and lows of 10 to 20 degrees Celsius.

Additionally, especially near the Gulf of Mexico and the Caribbean Sea, Mexico is vulnerable to seasonal weather events like hurricanes and tropical storms. Typically, the hurricane season lasts from June to November, with September and October seeing the most activity. These storms have the potential to produce high winds and heavy rain, which may cause infrastructure damage and floods.

It is important to note that there may be regional variances within these climatic zones as a result of Mexico's enormous size and diverse geography. For instance, mountainous areas include microclimates where temperature and precipitation patterns may differ greatly over short distances.

Mexico has a varied climate with unique seasonal patterns, ranging from tropical to temperate and dry. These climatic zones are a result of the country's diverse terrain, which provides travelers and locals with a broad diversity of weather conditions to enjoy all year long.

## Culture Of Mexico

The indigenous origins of its indigenous peoples, the impact of Spanish colonialism, and a complex fusion of traditions and practices that have developed over centuries have all contributed to Mexico's lively and diversified culture. The culture of Mexico is made up of many different aspects, such as language, religion, art, music, dance, food, and festivals.

Spanish is the official language of Mexico, and it plays a big part in the culture. Nahuatl, Maya, Zapotec, and Mixtec are just a few of the various indigenous languages that are spoken throughout the nation. The cultural legacy of

Mexico must be preserved via the development and preservation of indigenous languages.

Mexican culture is profoundly influenced by religion, with the vast majority of people identifying as Roman Catholics. In Mexico, Catholicism, and indigenous beliefs and rituals have coexisted to create a distinctive kind of religious syncretism. A complex tapestry of spiritual practices and beliefs is woven together by traditional indigenous rites and ceremonies and Catholic feasts.

Mexico's vibrant, colorful, and symbolic art is well known. Complex ceramics, stone sculptures, and paintings were made by ancient civilizations like the Maya and Aztec. Mexican art now spans a variety of aesthetics, from the famous paintings by Diego Rivera to the colorful folk art known as "arte popular." Mexican art is known for its use of vibrant colors and strong imagery, which reflects the country's vivacious personality.

Mexican culture is not complete without music and dancing. Traditional musical styles like mariachi, banda, ranchera, and cumbia instill a feeling of pride in one's country. The mariachi, a band of musicians that perform while donning traditional charro garb, is a representation of Mexican music. The rich cultural legacy of Mexico is celebrated via traditional dances like the Danzón and the Jarabe Tapato (Mexican Hat Dance).

Mexican food is recognized around the globe for its variety and tastes. It combines native ingredients with culinary innovations introduced by Spanish colonists. Corn, beans, chiles, tomatoes, avocados, and a variety of meats are common ingredients in Mexican food. Tacos, tamales, enchiladas, guacamole, and mole are just a handful of the mouthwatering foods that typify Mexican cuisine.

In Mexican culture, festivals and festivities have a particular position. The Day of the Dead (Da de los Muertos) is a well-known holiday in which families decorate colorful altars for their loved ones who have passed away, go to cemeteries, and participate in spirited processions. Another notable holiday is

Independence Day, which is observed on September 16 and honors Mexico's battle for independence from Spain. Festivals unite communities in joyful celebration via music, dancing, parades, fireworks, and local delicacies.

Mexican culture also places a high priority on close relationships with the community and family. Mexican culture places a strong emphasis on family, with extended relatives often living nearby and helping one another. Mexican culture has a strong feeling of belonging and tremendous respect for elders.

Mexicans are passionate about their ancestry and take pride in their country's identity. This patriotism is shown in the celebration of national icons like Frida Kahlo and Emiliano Zapata as well as the Mexican flag, eagle, and snake emblem.

Mexican culture has recently been more well-known and influential on the world stage because of its contributions to literature, cinema, and the arts. Mexican authors, painters, and filmmakers have made important contributions to their respective disciplines while presenting both the country's rich cultural history and modern viewpoints.

Mexican culture is a colorful synthesis of native customs, Spanish influences, and a youthful, modern attitude. It is distinguished by its wide range of artistic expressions, vibrant music and dance, delectable food, and deeply ingrained religious and communal traditions.

.

# CHAPTER TWO

## Visa Requirements To Visit Mexico

Foreign visitors to Mexico often need to apply for the proper visa depending on their intended use and intended length of stay. Depending on your country of citizenship and the expected duration of your trip, there may be different visa requirements for Mexico. For travel to Mexico, the following popular visa types are listed:

The Forma Migratoria Multiple (FMM), sometimes known as a tourist visa, is used by the majority of tourists to enter Mexico. This document, which is often granted upon arrival at the port of entry, permits visitors to remain in Mexico for up to 180 days (six months). Presenting a passport that is still valid and completing the required documentation will get you the FMM. The FMM card has to be returned upon departure, therefore it's crucial to have it with you the whole time you're there.

Visitor Visa (VME): Before your trip, you may need to get a Visitor Visa (VME) if you want to remain in Mexico for more than 180 days. This visa is appropriate for those traveling to Mexico to visit relatives, do business, or engage in short-term activities. The VME needs an application procedure and accompanying papers, including a current passport, evidence of financial capability, and justification for the travel. The VME might last anywhere from 180 days to a maximum of four years, depending on the circumstance.

Business Visa: You could need a business visa if you are visiting Mexico for professional purposes, such as meetings, conferences, or negotiations. This visa calls for an invitation letter from a Mexican corporation or organization and permits brief business visits. Consult the Mexican embassy or consulate in your country for more information on the criteria for a business visa since they may differ from country to country.

Student Visa: You must apply for a Student Visa (Residente Temporal Estudiante) if you want to study in Mexico. This kind of visa, which permits longer stays, is often given to students enrolled in reputable educational institutions. You will be asked to verify your admittance into a Mexican educational institution, evidence of your financial ability, and other necessary paperwork.

The most recent information may be found on the official website of the Mexican embassy or consulate in your country. It's crucial to remember that visa requirements might vary over time. Additionally, certain nationalities, such as nationals of nations taking part in the Visa Waiver Program, may not need a visa for short-term stays. These visitors may visit Mexico for leisure or business without a visa, but they'll still need to get an FMM when they get there.

To provide enough processing time, it is advised to apply for the necessary visa well before your anticipated trip dates. Entry may be refused, there may be penalties or even deportation for violating immigration and visa regulations in Mexico.

For the most precise and recent information on the need for a visa in your particular circumstance, remember to check official sources and get in touch with the Mexican embassy or consulate in your nation.

## Important things To Know Before Visiting Mexico

To guarantee a safe and pleasurable trip, it is crucial to be ready and aware of several factors before traveling to Mexico. When arranging a trip to Mexico, keep the following in mind:

- Although Mexico is a beautiful and friendly nation, it is crucial to take steps to secure your safety. Do your homework on the places you want to go and keep up with any travel warnings that your government has issued. Be careful with your possessions, avoid showing off your affluence, and choose safe transportation. It is best to travel in groups, especially at night or in uncharted territory.

- Spanish is the official language of Mexico. Even though English is widely spoken in tourist regions, knowing a few basic Spanish phrases can help you get about and converse with people.

- Currency: The Mexican Peso (MXN) is used as money in Mexico. For minor transactions and local markets, it is recommended to have some local money on hand. Most businesses take major credit cards, but it's always a good idea to have extra cash on hand, particularly in rural locations.

- Tipping customs: Tipping is expected in Mexico, especially in bars, restaurants, and for other services like taxis and hotel personnel. For great service, it is customary to leave a tip of at least 15% of the entire tab.

- Buses, taxis, and the metro are all part of Mexico's enormous transportation network, which also includes the country's biggest cities. For safety and to prevent fraud, it is advised to only utilize licensed taxi services or ride-hailing applications. It's crucial to use care and keep a watch on your items while using public transit since the quality and safety might vary widely.

- Mexico's climate varies considerably depending on the location. It's critical to check the weather forecast and prepare appropriately. High-altitude places may have lower temperatures, whereas coastal areas may have tropical or subtropical climates. For warmer climates, bring sunscreen, a hat, and lightweight, breathable clothes; for chilly climates, think about layering.

- Mexicans are often kind and hospitable, according to local customs and etiquette. Respect for regional norms and politeness is essential. It is polite to extend a handshake and say "por favor" (please) and "gracias" (thank you).

Before beginning to eat, it's usual to say "buen provecho" (enjoy your meal).

- Cultural Sensitivity: Due to Mexico's rich cultural legacy, it is crucial to respect regional traditions and customs. When visiting rural regions or religious locations, modest attire is preferred. Your experience may be improved by being familiar with and enjoying local traditions and customs.

- Mexican food is renowned for its tastes and spices and is both tasty and unique. Be daring and experiment with classic foods like tacos, tamales, mole, and fresh seafood. To prevent any possible health problems, it is advised to consume bottled water and to be careful while eating street food.

- Exploring Diversity: Mexico has a variety of things to offer, from historical sites like the Mayan ruins to lovely beaches, colonial villages, and bustling cities. According to your interests and the areas you want to see, do some research and arrange your schedule. Spend some time becoming acquainted with the Mexican way of life since it has a rich cultural and natural history.

It's important to keep in mind that experiences might differ depending on the location within Mexico, so it's best to do some research and talk to locals before you go. You may have a memorable and delightful trip to Mexico by planning beforehand, respecting local traditions, and being cautious.

## Best Time To Visit Mexico For The Best Experience

The optimal time to go to Mexico depends on several variables, including preferred weather, desired activities, and particular places of interest. Mexico is a year-round destination due to its varied temperature and geographical characteristics, however, there are several important factors to take into account while making travel arrangements:

The dry season (winter) and the wet season (summer) are the two main seasons of Mexico. Warm, pleasant weather with little rainfall defines the dry season, which lasts from November to April. This period is perfect for taking part in outdoor activities, seeing cultural attractions, and having fun at the beach. The rainy season, which lasts from May to October, raises temperatures and increases precipitation, especially in tropical and coastal areas. It's a terrific time to view the beautiful scenery and take advantage of less crowded tourist attractions since the rain showers are often light and may be followed by the bright sky.

High Tourism Season: The dry season and significant holidays usually fall during Mexico's peak tourism season. Due to Christmas, New Year's, and winter holidays, there is a spike in tourism throughout December and January in particular. Popular tourist spots like Cancun, the Riviera Maya, Puerto Vallarta, and Mexico City may be congested during this period, and hotel rates might be higher. Consider traveling in the off-peak months (April–May or

September–October) if you want a more relaxed experience and cheaper rates.

Beach & Coastal Activities: The Pacific Ocean, the Gulf of Mexico, and the Caribbean Sea all have beautiful beaches and coastal zones. Mexico is no exception. The dry season is a great time to come for beach lovers since the weather is often sunny and water sports like swimming, snorkeling, and diving are optimal. If you're considering a trip to the Caribbean at this time, make careful to keep an eye on weather predictions. The Caribbean coast may be more susceptible to hurricanes during this period.

Events of a Cultural and Festive Nature: Mexico is well known for its vibrant festivals and cultural festivities. Easter and Holy Week are important religious holidays that, although their dates change every year, typically take place in March or April. Another culturally significant holiday worth taking part in is Dia de los Muertos (Day of the Dead), which takes place in late October or early November. Major cultural festivals that include traditional music, dancing, and food include the Guelaguetza festival in Oaxaca (July) and the Feria Nacional de San Marcos in Aguascalientes (April-May).

Outdoor Adventures: The dry season is often preferable if you're interested in outdoor pursuits like hiking, discovering natural marvels, or seeing historical places. For activities like trekking in Copper Canyon, seeing historic Mayan sites on the Yucatán Peninsula, or discovering Chiapas' biosphere reserves, cooler temperatures in the mornings and nights are ideal.

Whale Watching: There are fantastic possibilities to see whales along Mexico's coastline. Depending on the area and kind of whale, different times of day are preferable for this activity. For instance, from December to April when gray whales pass through the area, Baja California and the Sea of Cortez are well-liked locations for whale watching. From December through March, humpback whales may be observed off the Pacific coast.

The ideal time to go to Mexico ultimately depends on your particular interests and the pursuits you want to make. Take into account the weather, local festivities, the number of visitors, and the particular places you wish to check out. You can maximize your time in Mexico and build priceless experiences by making thoughtful travel arrangements.

## Basic Spanish Phrases To Interact With The Locals

Having a few basic Spanish phrases at your disposal might be immensely beneficial while visiting a Spanish-speaking nation like Mexico. Even though English is often spoken in tourist regions, attempting to converse in the local tongue shows respect and may improve your trip. The following key Spanish expressions will enable you to communicate with the locals:

- Greetings and Polite Expressions:
- Hola - Hello
- Buenos días - Good morning

- Buenas tardes - Good afternoon
- Buenas noches - Good evening/night
- Por favor - Please
- Gracias - Thank you
- De nada - You're welcome
- Permiso - Excuse me
- Introductions:
- ¿Cómo te llamas? - What's your name?
- Me llamo... - My name is...
- Mucho gusto - Nice to meet you
- ¿Cómo estás? - How are you?
- Estoy bien, gracias - I'm fine, thank you
- ¿Y tú? - And you?
- Asking for Help:
- ¿Puedes ayudarme? - Can you help me?
- ¿Dónde está...? - Where is...?
- Necesito ayuda - I need help
- ¿Habla inglés? - Do you speak English?
- No entiendo - I don't understand
- ¿Puedes repetir, por favor? - Can you repeat, please?
- ¿Cómo se dice... en español? - How do you say... in Spanish?
- Ordering Food and Drinks:
- Quisiera... - I would like...

- La cuenta, por favor - The bill, please
- ¿Tienes recomendaciones? - Do you have any recommendations?
- ¿Qué es esto? - What is this?
- ¿Tienes un menú en inglés? - Do you have an English menu?
- ¿Puedo tener agua, por favor? - Can I have some water, please?
- ¿Cuánto cuesta? - How much does it cost?
- Directions and Transportation:
- ¿Cómo llego a...? - How do I get to...?
- ¿Dónde está la estación de autobuses? - Where is the bus station?
- ¿Dónde puedo tomar un taxi? - Where can I take a taxi?
- ¿Cuánto cuesta el boleto? - How much is the ticket?
- Está cerca/lejos - It's close/far
- Derecha - Right
- Izquierda - Left
- Shopping and Bargaining:
- ¿Cuánto cuesta? - How much does it cost?

- ¿Tienes esto en otro color/talla? - Do you have this in another color/size?
- ¿Puedes hacerme un descuento? - Can you give me a discount?
- ¿Aceptas tarjeta de crédito? - Do you accept credit cards?
- Está muy caro - It's too expensive
- ¿Cuál es tu mejor precio? - What 's your best price?
- Emergency Situations:
- Ayuda - Help
- ¡Llama a la policía! - Call the police!
- ¡Necesito un médico! - I need a doctor!
- ¡Perdí mi pasaporte! - I lost my passport!
- ¿Dónde está la embajada más cercana? - Where is the nearest embassy?
- ¡Fuego! - Fire!

Even if your Spanish is not perfect, always talk slowly and clearly. The locals will value your effort and could be more eager to assist you. Additionally, pointing or utilizing hand motions might be beneficial in

# Things To Bring Along On Your Trip To Mexico

Pack sensibly for your vacation to Mexico to guarantee a relaxing and delightful experience. The following things are crucial to bring:

- Valid Passport: Verify that your passport will be valid for at least six months after the date you want to travel. Keep a duplicate of your passport's front page separate from the original in case you need it in an emergency.

- Mexican Visa or Tourist Card: You could require a visa or tourist card (Forma Migratoria Multiple, FMM) to visit Mexico, depending on your nationality and the duration of your stay. Verify the criteria for your particular circumstance and carry the required documentation.

- Keep all of your important travel papers organized and simple to find. This includes any relevant immunization records, airline and hotel confirmations, and information about travel insurance.

- Carry a combination of cash and debit/credit cards for payments. Mexican Pesos (MXN) is commonly accepted, particularly at more intimate businesses and neighborhood markets. Additionally, let your bank know about your trip intentions so they can make sure your cards will operate abroad.

- Keep some Mexican Pesos on hand for little transactions, gratuities, and locations that may not take credit cards. Cash may be taken out of ATMs or exchanged at approved exchange offices.

- Travel insurance may help you guard against unexpected circumstances by paying for medical costs, trip cancellations, and personal effects. Make sure the insurance covers any activities you want to partake in, such as hiking or adventure sports, by checking.

- Bring any required prescription prescriptions in their original containers, as well as a copy of the prescription, along with a first aid kit. Pack a basic first aid package as well, including any personal drugs or cures, sticky bandages, antibacterial ointment, and pain relievers.

- Comfortable Clothes and Shoes: Bring breathable, light clothing that is appropriate for the environment and activities you want to participate in. For touring towns and ancient sites in Mexico, think about bringing clothes and sturdy walking shoes.

- Mexico utilizes Type A and Type B electrical outlets. Travel adapters and chargers are required. An appropriate converter and charger for your electrical gadgets should be brought.

- Pack sunscreen, a wide-brimmed hat, sunglasses, and a light, long-sleeved shirt for additional sun protection as the sun can be quite fierce in Mexico.

- Language Resources: To facilitate conversation, think about taking a small Spanish phrasebook or downloading a language app.

- Having a travel guidebook or maps of the places you want to visit may be useful for navigating and learning about the local attractions.

- Include personal safety devices like a lock for your baggage, a money belt or neck pouch for safeguarding valuables, and copies of any critical papers.

- Snacks and Water Bottle: To remain hydrated on lengthy flights, bring some snacks and a reusable water bottle. If the area's tap water is unsafe to consume, it is advised to drink bottled water or to use a water filter.

To properly pack, keep in mind to check the weather forecast and any special needs for your trip. You may have everything you need when traveling in Mexico by packing lightly and concentrating on the essentials.

# CHAPTER THREE

## Getting Around Mexico

Mexico provides a variety of transportation choices to accommodate diverse travel tastes and price ranges and is generally simple to navigate. Here are some tips for getting about the nation to improve your trip experience:

**1. Domestic Flights:** Travel between major cities and tourism hotspots is made easier by Mexico's well-established domestic aircraft network. Regular flights are provided by carriers with affordable fares, including Aeroméxico, Volaris, and Interjet. When traveling over great distances or swiftly reaching distant locations, domestic planes are very helpful.

**2. Buses:** In Mexico, buses are a common and cost-effective means of transportation. There is a vast bus network in the nation that links urban, suburban, and even rural locations.

First-class and executive buses with facilities like air conditioning, onboard restrooms, and Wi-Fi are available from reputable bus companies like ADO, ETN, and Primera Plus. These buses are pleasant and dependable. When traveling at a premium, think about making reservations in advance.

**3. Public transportation and the metro:** Mexico City and a few other significant cities have effective metro systems that make it simple to go about. The second-largest metro area in North America is Mexico City, and it provides a cheap means of getting about the city. In metropolitan areas, public buses and minibusses, often known as "peseros," are common and provide a cheap form of transportation. It should be noted, nevertheless, that during rush hours, public transportation might become congested and less dependable.

**4. Rental cars:** If you want to visit rural locations or want a more autonomous travel experience, renting a vehicle allows you the opportunity to explore at your speed. At airports and in major cities, a wide variety of foreign and local vehicle rental firms supply their services. It's crucial to know the traffic laws and road conditions in Mexico and to have a valid driver's license. Drive with caution while in congested metropolitan areas.

**5. Taxis and ride-hailing** services are readily accessible in Mexico, although it is advised to only utilize licensed taxi services, such as those that may be hailed from recognized taxi stands or by respected businesses. Uber and Didi are two well-liked ride-hailing applications that provide a simple and safe method to move around major cities.

**6. Trains:** Although there are a few prominent beautiful rail routes in Mexico, there isn't as much train travel as there is in other countries. The most well-known of them is the Chihuahua al Pacifico (Chepe) railway, which traverses the Copper Canyon area and provides stunning vistas. For those who want to immerse themselves in Mexico's breathtaking scenery, this train trip is a fantastic choice.

**7. Ferries:** To reach surrounding islands and coastal locations, ferries are available from Mexico's coastal areas, including the Yucatán Peninsula, Baja California, and the Gulf of California. Ferries may be a terrific way to go to locations like Cozumel, Isla Mujeres, or Baja California Sur, where you can take part in water sports like snorkeling and enjoy beautiful beaches.

**8. Walking and Biking:** Especially in locations with bike lanes and pedestrian-friendly infrastructure, exploring Mexico's cities and towns on foot or by bicycle may be a great way to see them. Rental bicycles are available at many tourist spots, and some towns also provide guided bike tours, which give an engaging and different way to see the local way of life and attractions.

Safety must be taken into account while traveling in Mexico. When traveling by public transportation, use care, be aware of your surroundings, and watch your possessions closely. Use trustworthy services, do your research on the standing of the transportation companies, and where required, get local guidance.

You can efficiently organize your schedule, see Mexico's many areas, and make your trip to the nation memorable by being aware of the transportation alternatives accessible.

## Practical Steps To Stay Safe In Mexico

Mexico is a dynamic and alluring location, but just like everywhere else, you need to exercise care to protect your safety and well-being while there. You may travel safely and successfully in Mexico by taking these useful steps:

- Study and Prepare in Advance: Educate yourself about the places you want to visit before your trip. Keep abreast of travel warnings and educate yourself on regional traditions, laws, and cultural standards. You may make wise judgments and reduce risks by using this information.

- Select trustworthy Accommodations: Opt for trustworthy lodgings, such as highly rated hotels or inns that place a premium on security. Look for amenities like round-the-clock surveillance, reliable locks, and well-lit entrances. Think about residing in tourist hotspots or locations with a solid reputation for safety.

- Use dependable modes of transportation, such as authorized taxis, ride-sharing services, or renowned tour operators. Avoid utilizing unauthorized or unmarked cabs, particularly after dark. Be careful in crowded areas and watch your things while using public transit.

- Personal Property: At all times, keep your valuables protected, such as passports, money, and devices. To carry your valuables and cash, use a money belt or a covert pouch. Don't wear flashy jewelry or carry extraneous things that can draw attention.

- Keep an eye out for Pickpockets and Petty Thieves in Crowded Areas: Mexico's major tourist destinations might be busy, making it easier for them to operate. Keep your baggage close to your body, pay attention to your surroundings, and never leave anything unattended.

- Dress modestly and make an effort to fit in with the community to avoid attracting unwanted attention. Keep costly objects and big quantities of cash out of sight. It will be easier to have a good experience if you are courteous and conscious of the regional traditions and customs.

- Make sure you have access to dependable communication, such as a local SIM card or a portable Wi-Fi device, to stay connected. By doing this, you'll be able to remain in touch with your traveling companions and, in an emergency, have access to emergency contacts and maps.

- Drink Sensibly: If you decide to partake in alcohol consumption, do it sensibly. Never leave your drink alone and be wary about taking beverages from strangers. Drinking too much might cloud your judgment and leave you open to fraud or dangerous circumstances.

- Use Caution When Eating Street Cuisine: Although Mexico is known for its mouthwatering street cuisine, it's crucial to make informed decisions. Choosing booths or sellers with a high turnover can ensure that the food is both fresh and safe. Be on the lookout for spotless kitchens, and make sure the food is fully cooked before eating.

- Your intuition is a great tool, so trust it. Whenever anything seems dangerous or uneasy, follow your gut and get out of the situation. Avoid going for solitary strolls in remote regions, particularly at night. Travel in groups or with a reliable companion, if at all feasible.

Keep in mind that, in addition to exercising caution, you should also savor and appreciate Mexico's natural beauty and kind friendliness. You may have a safe and enjoyable time discovering this amazing country's marvels by following this sensible advice and being informed.

## Do's And Don'ts In Mexico

To show respect and guarantee a pleasant trip, it's crucial to get acquainted with the regional traditions and etiquette before visiting Mexico. The following are some things to remember:

**Do's**:

- Although English is often spoken in tourist regions, making an effort to learn a few fundamental Spanish words will help you communicate with the people.

- Greeting others Politeness is important to Mexicans since they esteem both. When entering stores or greeting people, say "Hola" (hello) or "Buenos das/tardes/noches" (good morning, afternoon, or evening).

- Use "Por Favor" and "Gracias": When conversing with locals, use "por favor" (please) and "gracias" (thank you). In Mexican culture, politeness is highly valued.

- Try the local cuisine: Mexican cuisine is well known for being wonderful. Try some of the regional cuisine, including tacos, enchiladas, tamales, and guacamole. Be daring and investigate different street food vendors, but choose those with clean facilities.

- Negotiate in Markets: In Mexico, market negotiations are prevalent. Price haggling is acceptable, particularly when buying handicrafts, souvenirs, or items at a local market. Be courteous and pleasant during the negotiation.

- Mexico is home to a large number of historical and cultural attractions. When visiting temples, ruins, or churches, abide by the norms and restrictions. Respect any clothing rules and be respectful of regional cultures.

- Explore Areas Other Than Tourist Attractions: While visiting well-known tourist hotspots is worthwhile, think about going off the beaten track to take in the local culture and lesser-known sights. Greater insight into Mexican life may be gained through interacting with residents in smaller towns and rural regions.

**Don'ts**:

- Don't consume Tap Water: In Mexico, it's typically a good idea to consume bottled water. Avoid drinking or brushing your teeth with tap water. Stick to bottled water, and when you buy, make sure the seal is still in place.

-

- Avoid flashing costly items like jewelry, cameras, or big sums of cash in public. To reduce the danger of theft, it is advisable to keep your valuables concealed and protected.

- You shouldn't assume that everyone understands English just because it's spoken in tourist areas. You shouldn't expect that everyone you come across will be able to speak English well. When required, utilize gestures together with basic Spanish to communicate.

- Avoid Overindulging in Alcohol: Drinking too much alcohol may impair judgment and leave you open to fraud or dangerous circumstances. Drink sensibly and pay attention to your surroundings, particularly while traveling to new places.

- Respect Religious Symbols: Catholicism is a vital part of Mexico's rich religious history. When visiting temples or other religious buildings, show reverence.

Avoid acting disrespectfully or taking pictures in off-limits locations.

- Avoid Littering: Mexico's natural beauty is a treasure, so do your part to protect it by refraining from littering. Respect the environment and properly dispose of your rubbish. Recycle or dispose of garbage according to any established procedures.

- Avoid Talking About Sensitive Subjects: Unless you have a close connection and feel comfortable doing so, stay away from talking about sensitive subjects like politics, religion, or divisive historical events. Respect other points of view and participate in discussions with an open mind.

# CHAPTER FOUR

## *Interesting Things To Do In Mexico*

Visitors may partake in a wide range of thrilling and interesting activities in Mexico, a dynamic and diversified nation. Mexico has much to offer everyone, from its incredible natural beauty to its delectable food and rich cultural legacy. Here are a few of the most intriguing activities in Mexico.

- Exploring Mexico's historic ruins and archaeological sites is one of its top attractions. Chichen Itza, one of the New Seven Wonders of the World and a UNESCO World Heritage site, is the most well-known location. The famous El Castillo pyramid, sometimes called the Temple of Kukulcan, can be seen in this historic Mayan city. Other noteworthy ruins are Tulum, set on a cliff overlooking the azure Caribbean Sea, and Palenque tucked away deep among the luxuriant forests of Chiapas.

- Mexico provides beautiful scenery and natural attractions for nature lovers. The Mesoamerican Barrier Reef, the second-largest coral reef system in the world and an excellent place for snorkeling and scuba diving, is found in the Riviera Maya and is known for its magnificent white sand beaches, pristine cenotes (natural sinkholes), and stunning landscape. A collection of steep valleys in the Mexican state of Chihuahua, known as the Copper Canyon, rival the Grand Canyon in terms of beauty and size. You may explore the canyon by strolling the beautiful paths or enjoying the thrilling Chepe train excursion.

- Food aficionados will enjoy Mexico's gastronomic landscape. Each area of Mexico has its characteristics, making Mexican food immensely varied. In the lively marketplaces of Mexico City, savor delectable street cuisine including tacos al pastor, tamales, and churros. Rich mole sauces and traditional tlayudas, which are big tortillas topped with different fillings, are also hallmarks of Oaxaca. Try cochinita pibil (slow-roasted pork) when visiting the Yucatan Peninsula to experience the distinctive tastes of Mayan food.

- Mexico's colonial towns provide a window into the country's colonial history. The towering Metropolitan Cathedral and Zocalo Plaza in Mexico City's historic core are both included on the UNESCO World Heritage List. San Miguel de Allende is a charming town in central Mexico that is well-known for its colonial architecture, vibrant streets, and vibrant art scene. Guanajuato is another lovely colonial jewel, with its colorful streets and subterranean tunnels.

- In Mexico, there are many exhilarating activities available for adventurers. Swim and take in the stunning stalactite and stalagmite formations as you explore the Yucatan Peninsula's Rio Secreto subterranean river system. Since gray whales come to Baja California's Pacific coast during the winter, there are wonderful possibilities to go whale watching there. In Sayulita, Puerto Escondido, or at the well-known breakers in Baja California, surfers may catch the waves.

- Mexico's lively customs and indigenous origins are reflected in its rich cultural legacy. Experience the Day of the Dead celebrations in Oaxaca, where the streets are alive with parades, altars, and bright decorations in memory of the dead. In Veracruz, behold the spellbinding spectacle of the Voladores de Papantla (Papantla Flyers), where performers spin from a tall pole while fastened by ropes.

Last but not least, you may sample and learn about Mexico's world-famous tequila and mezcal in its distilleries. Take a tour of the Jalisco tequila-producing area and stop by distilleries to see how Mexico's national beverage is made. Discover the many types and aromas of this smokey agave-based liqueur by touring mezcal producers in Oaxaca.

# Historical Sites To See In Mexico

Mexico is a privileged nation with a fascinating and rich past, and it is home to some of the most incredible historical sites on earth. Mexico provides a wide range of locations that enable travelers to dig into its colorful history and see the remains of incredible civilizations, from historic towns to antiquated ruins.

- Chichen Itza, an ancient Mayan city situated on the Yucatan Peninsula, is one of Mexico's most breathtaking historical monuments. Chichen Itza, one of the New Seven Wonders of the World and a UNESCO World Heritage site, captivates with its majestic architecture. El Castillo, the famous Kukulcan Pyramid, which towers over the surrounding area, was built precisely to coincide with astronomical phenomena. Additional wonders to discover are the Great Ball Court, the Temple of the Warriors, and the holy Cenote Sagrado (holy Cenote), each of which offers insights into the enthralling Mayan civilization.

- Another fascinating historical monument that provides insight into Mexico's ancient history is Teotihuacan, which is close to Mexico City. During its heyday in the first to seventh century AD, this pre-Columbian metropolis was one of the biggest in the world. Teotihuacan is most known for its magnificent Pyramids of the Sun and Moon, the latter of which is the third-largest pyramid in the world. Visitors may explore the Temple of the Feathered Serpent, which is embellished with elaborate sculptures, as well as the well-preserved apartment complexes while strolling down the Avenue of the Dead. These sites provide a fascinating look into the everyday life of the Teotihuacan people.

- Palenque, a city tucked away in Chiapas's forests, is a magnificent example of the splendor of the pre-Columbian Maya culture. Beautiful architectural buildings embellished with dexterous sculptures and hieroglyphics may be seen at the Palenque archaeological site. Due to the presence of a tomb allegedly belonging to the renowned Maya king Pakal the Great, the Temple of the Inscriptions is especially remarkable. Visitors may explore the location and get engrossed in the magical ambiance of this old city, which is surrounded by lush flora and the howling of monkeys.

- Another amazing historical location that enthralls tourists with its beauty and cultural history is Guanajuato, a colonial jewel in central Mexico. The city's vibrant colonial structures, narrow lanes, and charming plazas take tourists back in time to the days of the Spanish colonial empire. Numerous creative events are held in the magnificent Juarez Theater, a cultural treasure with neoclassical architecture. A romantic tale is associated with the lovely, small Callejon del Beso (Alley of the Kiss). A former grain exchange turned museum, the Alhondiga de Granaditas, also depicts the tale of Guanajuato's major contribution to the Mexican War of Independence.

- Numerous historical treasures may be found in Mexico City. The major temple of the ancient Aztec capital of Tenochtitlan was previously located at the archaeological site known as the Templo Mayor, which is situated in the middle of the city's historic district. Excavations have uncovered several layers of history, illustrating how the location has changed through time. One of the biggest and oldest churches in the Americas, the Metropolitan Cathedral is an architectural wonder and is located next to the Templo Mayor. Its construction, which took more than 250 years, exhibits a fusion of architectural styles.

To sum up, Mexico has a ton of magnificent historical landmarks that provide a window into its fascinating and varied history. These locations let tourists fully immerse themselves in Mexico's cultural history, from the magnificence of Chichen Itza and Teotihuacan to the ethereal remains of Palenque and the colonial charm of Guanajuato.

# Top Museums And Galleries In Mexico

Mexico is home to a broad variety of outstanding museums that highlight its interesting history and rich cultural heritage. These museums provide a wide variety of exhibitions that appeal to different interests, ranging from ancient civilizations to modern art. Some of Mexico's best museums are listed below:

One of the best anthropological museums in the world is the National Museum of Anthropology (Museo Nacional de Antropologa) in Mexico City. It has a sizable collection of relics from Mexico's pre-Columbian cultures, including those of the Aztecs, Maya, and Olmec. Impressive exhibits in the museum provide light on the customs, ideals, and accomplishments of these antiquated civilizations. The legendary Aztec Sun Stone, also called the Stone of the Five Eras and representing the Aztec cosmology, serves as the centerpiece.

The Blue House, or La Casa Azul, is another name for the Frida Kahlo Museum, which is situated in Mexico City's Coyoacán district. Frida Kahlo, a well-known Mexican artist, has lived there in the past. The museum provides a look into Kahlo's life, work, and possessions. Visitors may tour her studio, view her famous works of art, and learn more about her distinctive creative style and the impact she had on Mexican art and culture.

In Mexico City, right next to the Templo Mayor archaeological site, lies the Templo Mayor

Museum (Museo del Templo Mayor). It displays the findings obtained during the excavation of Tenochtitlan, the Aztec capital. Intricate stone sculptures, ceremonial items, and gifts are among the museum's displays that provide light on the religious customs and rituals of the Aztec civilization. The museum also has a thorough description of the Templo Mayor's history and importance.

The stunningly attractive Soumaya Museum (Museo Soumaya) in Mexico City is home to a sizable collection of artwork from many historical eras and artistic movements. The museum, which bears Carlos Slim's late wife's name, has more than 66,000 items on display, including works by European artists like Van Gogh, Rodin, and Monet as well as a noteworthy collection of Mexican art. The museum stands out as a landmark in the city because of its distinctive architectural style, which is defined by its reflecting façade.

In Mexico City's Chapultepec Castle, the National Museum of History (Museo Nacional de Historia) is situated. Pre-Hispanic periods to the present are covered by the museum. Key historical occurrences including the Spanish conquest, the Mexican War of Independence, and the Mexican Revolution are covered in the exhibitions. The museum's interior features lavish spaces that were formerly used by Mexican royalty, providing a window into the period of colonial authority.

These are only a handful of Mexico's best museums, each of which provides a unique and educational cultural experience. Mexico's museums provide a plethora of information and creative appreciation for tourists to explore, whether they are interested in ancient civilizations, contemporary art, or the history of the nation.

## Parks And Gardens In Mexico

Mexico is endowed with a wide variety of parks and gardens that provide a break from the busy city life and highlight the beauty of the land. Mexico's outdoor areas provide chances for leisure, entertainment, and discovery, from beautiful botanical gardens to vast national parks.

One of the biggest urban parks in the world, Chapultepec Park (Bosque de Chapultepec) in Mexico City is made up of more than 1,600 acres. Within the busy capital city, this enormous green haven provides a tranquil refuge. The popular National Museum of Anthropology, Chapultepec Castle, and the Chapultepec Zoo are just a few of the attractions that can be found inside the park. The park's lake offers visitors the opportunity to take leisurely paddleboat rides, eat by the water's edge, and wander along tree-lined trails.

In the south of Mexico City, there is a UNESCO World Heritage site called Xochimilco. Xochimilco, which is well-known for its system of canals, gives guests a unique experience where they may board colorful trajineras (traditional boats) and float around the waterways surrounded by floating gardens, or chinampas. These floating gardens are landscaped areas where food, flowers, and other plants are planted. The quiet and gorgeous location of Xochimilco is ideal for taking a leisurely boat trip, viewing the bright vegetation, and taking in traditional Mexican culture.

The Ethnobotanical Garden (Jardn Etnobotánico) in the city of Oaxaca displays the extensive plant variety in the area. The garden's mission is to preserve and inform visitors about the customary usage of plants by Oaxacan indigenous groups. Visitors may find a vast range of native plants while strolling around the garden, including ceremonial plants, culinary components, and medicinal herbs. To encourage sustainable practices and cultural awareness, the garden also conducts seminars and educational events.

The Copper Canyon (Barranca del Cobre) in the Mexican state of Chihuahua is a must-see location for nature lovers. Outdoor recreation options abound in this huge canyon system, which is deeper and bigger than the Grand Canyon. There are numerous national parks in the Copper Canyon, including the Basaseachi Waterfall National Park and the Copper Canyon

National Park. Popular methods to explore the breathtaking vistas and fully immerse oneself in the region's natural beauties include hiking, horseback riding, and taking the beautiful Ferrocarril Chihuahua al Pacfico train excursion.

The coastal regions of Mexico also include lovely gardens and parks. On the Yucatan Peninsula's Caribbean coast, the Tulum National Park mixes breathtaking coastline scenery with prehistoric Mayan ruins. Visitors may stroll around the well-restored ruins that overlook the turquoise ocean before unwinding on the immaculate white sand beaches. Another protected region in the Yucatan Peninsula is the Sian Ka'an Biosphere Reserve, which includes a variety of habitats such as mangroves, wetlands, and barrier reefs. The reserve is a great place for kayaking, snorkeling, and birding, giving visitors the chance to get close to nature and see the richness of the area.

Mexico's parks and gardens provide a serene haven and an opportunity to take in the beauty of the country's natural landscape, whether it's a leisurely walk through a botanical garden, a boat trip along canals, or an adventure in a national park. These outdoor places provide something for everyone to enjoy and experience the grandeur of Mexico's landscapes, from pure natural reserves to urban green spaces.

# CHAPTER FIVE

## Shopping In Mexico

The retail environment in Mexico is vibrant and diverse, offering a choice of options to suit all tastes and budgets. Mexico has a lot to offer, from thriving artisan markets to upscale shopping malls.

One of the most well-known places to shop in Mexico is the local markets. You may buy a variety of handicrafts, traditional textiles, pottery, and jewelry in Mexico City's Mercado de la Ciudadela. It's the perfect place to learn about Mexican culture firsthand and discover one-of-a-kind presents. The Mercado de Benito Juarez in Oaxaca is widely recognized for its wide selection of native products, which includes handcrafted textiles, ethnic clothing, and vibrant pottery. Mexico's markets are not only places to purchase things; they are also lively cultural hubs where visitors can interact with local artisans and learn about their way of life.

The main cities in Mexico provide a broad selection of modern shopping malls and expensive stores for those seeking elite shopping experiences. The wealthy Polanco neighborhood of Mexico City is home to high-end luxury stores including Louis Vuitton, Gucci, and Chanel. The Santa Fe Shopping Center, one of Latin America's largest malls, has a range of luxury brands, international retailers, and entertainment options. Cancun's Luxury Avenue showcases well-known brands in a breathtaking beachfront setting, offering a high-end shopping experience.

Mexico is well-known for its silver jewelry, and cities like Taxco are well-known for manufacturing silver. The various silver shops and workshops in Taxco, which is in the state of Guerrero, sell intricate products created by gifted artisans. Every year, the city has a silver fair that attracts tourists from all over the world who like jewelry.

Additionally, Mexico is also known for its vibrant street markets, where vendors sell a variety of goods, including clothing, accessories, handicrafts, and food. San Juan Market in Mexico City, which provides a wide range of gourmet delights, including fresh vegetables, spices, and regional delicacies, is a must-visit for food lovers.

Whether you're looking for regional foods, high-end clothing, or traditional crafts, shopping in Mexico provides a diverse and entertaining experience. From ancient markets to modern malls, the country's retail landscape reflects its rich cultural heritage and offers something for every kind of consumer to enjoy.

# Events And Festivals In Mexico

Mexico is a nation rich in cultural traditions and festivals, with events taking place all year round. Mexico provides a wide variety of events and festivals that highlight the nation's distinctive character and history, ranging from religious celebrations to vibrant carnivals. The following are a few of the most well-liked occasions and festivals in Mexico:

- **Da de los Muertos, or Day of the Dead**

   The Day of the Dead event, which celebrates the remembrance of departed loved ones, is one of Mexico's most well-known celebrations. This celebration, which is observed on November 1st and 2nd, involves altars decorated in bright colors, sugar skulls, and traditional delicacies like pan de muerto (bread of the dead). With ceremonies ranging from somber processions to boisterous parties, the holiday is a time for families to gather together and commemorate their loved ones.

- **Carnival**

Pre-Lenten holiday known as Carnival is observed across Mexico's cities, with some of the most well-known events taking place in Veracruz, Mazatlan, and Ensenada. Participants dance in the streets to the sounds of traditional music throughout the event, which is characterized by vibrant parades, upbeat music, and spectacular costumes. Carnival is a time to have fun and relax before the austere season of Lent starts.

- **Guelaguetza**

Every year, the city of Oaxaca hosts the Guelaguetza festival to honor the indigenous cultures and customs of the area. The event showcases local culture via its participants' traditional dances, music, and cuisine. The event is a must-see for anybody interested in

Mexican culture and draws tourists from all over the globe.

- **Holiday of Independence (Da de la Independencia)**

Mexico's Independence Day, observed on September 16 to commemorate the nation's independence from Spain in 1810, is a national holiday. Colorful parades, fireworks, and concerts are held to commemorate the festival, and people congregate in town squares to do so. The Cry of Independence (El Grito), during which the Mexican president joins the audience in chanting "Viva Mexico!" and striking the National Palace bell, is the most well-known event.

- **Festival of the Candle**

The state of Veracruz's town of Tlacotalpan honors its patron saint at the Festival de la Candelaria. Participants in the celebration wear traditional attire and carry statues of the Virgin of Candelaria

as they parade through the streets to the sounds of live music and dancing. The celebration, which blends Catholic and indigenous customs,
highlights the region's rich cultural legacy.

- **The San Marcos Fair**

The city of Aguascalientes hosts the Feria de San Marcos every year to honor the town's patron saint. Visitors from all across the nation converge on the city for the celebrations, which include a variety of events including bullfights, music, and carnival rides. With nearly seven million attendees annually, the Feria de San Marcos is one of Mexico's biggest and most well-known events.

- **the fifth of May**

The Mexican army's triumph against the French at the Battle of Puebla in 1862 is commemorated on May 5th or Cinco de Mayo. The majority of the world's celebrations take place in the United States, where it has come to symbolize Mexican-American culture. Although it is not a significant holiday in Mexico, certain states do have parades and festivities to mark the occasion.

In conclusion, Mexico is a nation that enjoys partying, and there are a ton of occasions and celebrations that highlight its rich cultural past. Mexico has plenty to offer everyone, from age-old traditions like the Day of the Dead and Guelaguetza to cutting-edge occasions like the Feria de San Marcos. Mexico's events and festivals provide a lively, whether you're seeking music, dancing, gastronomy, or culture.

## Nightlife In Mexico

The vibrant, exciting, and diverse nightlife in Mexico is well known for providing a broad variety of entertainment alternatives for night owls. Mexico's nightlife industry has something for everyone, from energetic nightclubs to quiet pubs and traditional music venues.

There are several alternatives for a flourishing nightlife in Mexico City. Popular nightclubs, elegant lounges, and trendy bars can be found in the areas of Polanco, Condesa, and Roma. In these locations, you may find a range of live music venues, DJ performances, and themed parties that include music ranging from electronic to Latin sounds. The city also has a long history of live music, with venues hosting performances of mariachi, salsa, and other classic Mexican musical genres.

On the Yucatan Peninsula, Cancun and Playa del Carmen are well known for their vibrant nightlife. While Playa del Carmen's renowned Fifth Avenue provides a bustling scene with bars, clubs, and street performers, the Hotel Zone in Cancun is home to countless nightclubs where international DJs play the newest songs. Beach parties and music festivals are also held in these vacation spots, drawing revelers from all over the globe.

On Mexico's Pacific coast, Puerto Vallarta is renowned for its thriving LGBTQ+ nightlife.

The vibrant selection of pubs, clubs, and drag performances in the city's Romantic Zone contribute to the area's accepting and inclusive vibe. Puerto Vallarta provides a wide variety of places that suit all tastes, from raucous dance floors to relaxed lounges.

Smaller villages and coastal locations in Mexico can provide distinctive nightlife experiences, in addition to the busy hubs. Visitors may savor beachside bars and clubs in Cabo San Lucas with breathtaking Pacific Ocean views. In addition to hosting well-known beach parties, Tulum in the Riviera Maya provides a bohemian vibe with seaside bars and live music performances.

Visits to cantinas, which are traditional taverns where residents congregate to enjoy beverages, tapas, and lively discussion, are part of the traditional nightlife in Mexico. These cantinas often include live music, and customers can enjoy regional libations like tequila or mezcal while soaking up the warm and vibrant environment.

When taking in Mexico's nightlife, safety is a crucial factor. Stick to well-known and respected locations, take safety measures, and pay attention to your personal property. Respecting local laws and norms around drinking and conduct is also crucial.

The nightlife culture in Mexico is diverse, with everything from lively clubs to tranquil pubs and traditional music venues. Mexico's nightlife offers something for everyone to enjoy long into the early hours of the morning, whether you're looking for lively dance floors, live music performances, or a laid-back evening with friends.

# CHAPTER SIX

## Budget Friendly Hotels In Mexico

Travelers searching for inexpensive lodging without sacrificing comfort and convenience may find several economical hotel alternatives in Mexico. There are many affordable hotels to choose from around the nation, whether you're touring the energetic cities, unwinding on the stunning beaches, or experiencing the rich cultural legacy.

- In Mexico City, the nation's capital and center of culture, you can discover a wide range of inexpensive hotels in areas like Zona Rosa, Roma, and Condesa. These regions are renowned for their lively energy, hip restaurants, and pubs. Guesthouses, hostels, and low-cost hotels are examples of budget-friendly lodging choices that provide tidy, pleasant rooms at reasonable prices. Hotels like Hotel Cartagena, Hotel Templo Mayor, and

Hotel Catedral are some well-liked low-cost accommodations in Mexico City.

- There are several inexpensive hotels in beach resorts like Cancun and Playa del Carmen that provide simple access to lovely beaches and exciting nightlife. These hotels often include standard services like spotless rooms, cost-free Wi-Fi, and in some cases, breakfast. The Hotel Antillano and Hotel Tankah are two examples of Cancun accommodations that are reasonably priced. Budget hotels in Playa del Carmen include Hotel Las Golondrinas and Hotel Labnah.

- Numerous other well-known tourist locations, like Oaxaca, Tulum, and Puerto Vallarta, also provide inexpensive lodging alternatives. Affordable hotels in Puerto Vallarta may be found in the Romantic Zone, near the city's thriving nightlife and the beach. For guests on a tight budget, hotels like Hotel Eloisa and

Hotel Posada de Roger are popular alternatives. Budget-friendly eco-friendly hotels and hostels like Mama's Home Tulum and Papaya Playa Project may be found in Tulum, a city famous for its beautiful beaches and Mayan ruins.

- In the ancient heart of Oaxaca, a city rich in cultural history and gastronomic pleasures, you may find inexpensive lodging. Both the Hotel Marqués del Valle and Hostal de las Américas are well-liked choices with cozy accommodations at reasonable prices.

- Because they often provide reduced prices and exclusive deals, think about making your hotel reservations via online travel agencies or hotel booking websites to save even more money. Planning your vacation during the off-peak or off-year when costs are often lower is also a smart idea.

Overall, Mexico has a large selection of inexpensive hotels that are geared toward budget-conscious tourists. You may discover inexpensive lodging that offers comfort, convenience, and fantastic value for your money in busy cities, gorgeous beaches, and cultural locations. You may have a fun-filled experience in Mexico without going over budget with proper preparation and study.

## Mid-range Hotels In Mexico

Several intermediate hotels in Mexico provide affordable, pleasant lodging to tourists. There are many alternatives available around the nation, whether you're seeking a beachside resort or a strategically situated hotel in a busy metropolis.

- In Mexico City, the nation's capital and center of culture, you can find midrange hotels in areas like Polanco, Zona Rosa, and Roma. As well as being close to popular sites, these districts are renowned for their chic restaurants, pubs, and shopping. In Mexico City, midrange hotels often include facilities including restaurants, rooftop pools, and fitness centers. The Hotel Geneve Ciudad de México, Hotel Marlowe, and Hotel Suites Amberes are a few examples of well-liked intermediate accommodations in Mexico City.

- Mid Range hotels are often found in great beachfront positions in beach resorts like Cancun, Playa del Carmen, and Puerto Vallarta and provide facilities including pools, restaurants, and spas. Krystal Cancun Hotel, Royal Solaris Cancun, and Emporio Cancun are a few examples of moderate accommodations in Cancun. The Playa Palms Beach Hotel and Aventura Mexicana Hotel are two examples of moderate accommodations in Playa del Carmen. Additionally, intermediate lodging options in Puerto Vallarta include Crown Paradise Golden Puerto Vallarta and Fiesta Americana Puerto Vallarta.

- The same is true of other well-known locations including Tulum, Guadalajara, and Oaxaca. Midrange lodgings in Tulum often provide eco-friendly practices and extras like beach access, yoga sessions, and spa services. Casa Malca and Ahau Tulum are two examples of midscale hotels in Tulum. Midrange accommodations in Guadalajara include the Hotel Morales Historical & Colonial Downtown Core and the Hotel Riu Plaza Guadalajara. For tourists seeking comfort and convenience in Oaxaca, midrange hotels like Hotel Casa Divina Oaxaca and Hotel Los Olivos Spa are excellent options.

Overall, Mexico has a large selection of mid-range hotels that are ideal for tourists seeking cozy lodgings at affordable prices. For visitors looking for a mix between comfort and budget, these hotels provide a terrific bargain with facilities like pools, restaurants, and fitness centers. Consider your location, desired facilities, and spending limit to discover the ideal midrange hotel for your requirements.

Then, book your stay via a dependable travel website or directly with the hotel.

## *Luxury Hotels In Mexico*

Mexico is well known for its opulent lodgings that provide top-notch facilities, first-rate service, and breathtaking scenery. Mexico's luxury hotels provide a genuinely sumptuous experience for discriminating guests, from coastal resorts to city getaways.

- Luxury resorts surround the beautiful Caribbean Sea shoreline in beach resorts like Cancun and Riviera Maya, providing breathtaking ocean vistas and opulent facilities. The luxurious accommodations, spa, several restaurants, and exclusive beach club of The Ritz-Carlton Cancun, which is situated on a lovely length of beach, are available. A championship golf course, opulent villas with private pools, and a renowned spa are all features of the

Riviera Maya resort The Banyan Tree Mayakoba.

- Luxury resorts in Los Cabos mix the splendor of the Sea of Cortez with breathtaking desert scenery. On a secluded beach, the One&Only Palmilla offers luxurious rooms and villas, top-notch dining choices, and a well-known spa. The Cape, a Thompson Hotel, provides chic lodgings, a rooftop bar, and easy access to one of the greatest surf breakers in the vicinity.

- Luxury hotels that appeal to discriminating guests may be found in Mexico City. In the posh Polanco district of Mexico City, St. Regis provides opulent accommodations with breathtaking city views, a luxurious spa, and fine dining choices. The Four Seasons Mexico City offers opulent rooms, a rooftop patio, and a famous spa. It is housed in a stunning colonial-style edifice.

- Luxury boutique hotels in San Miguel de Allende's historic district provide a refined and personal setting. The Hotel Matilda boasts modern architecture, a spa, a rooftop pool, and an art gallery. Rosewood San Miguel de Allende has an architecture with colonial influences, lovely gardens, and opulent lodgings with fireplaces and patios.

- Several opulent resorts that combine elegance and the unspoiled beauty of the Pacific coast may be found in Puerto Vallarta. Private beaches, roomy casitas, and world-class golf courses are all features of the Four Seasons Resort Punta Mita. One&Only Mandarina offers gorgeous cliffside villas, a spa, and expansive ocean views while being tucked away in a natural jungle environment.

- The Hacienda Chichen Resort at Chichen Itza, on the Yucatan Peninsula, offers a luxurious and tranquil getaway next to the well-known Mayan ruins. The resort provides access to the archaeological site, tastefully renovated accommodations, and an organic spa. The Rosewood Mayakoba on the Riviera Maya, farther south, provides opulent suites and villas tucked away in a beautiful tropical setting, as well as a private beach and a championship golf course.

These are just a few examples of the opulent lodging options available in Mexico. Mexico's luxury hotels provide a degree of care, comfort, and magnificence that will beyond your expectations, whether you're looking for a seaside hideaway, a downtown paradise, or a historic hacienda. Experience Mexico's rich cultural history, feast on the cuisine of the highest caliber, and unwind in opulence at one of the best five-star hotels in the nation.

## Camping In Mexico

Mexico's varied landscapes, from its clean beaches and lush rainforests to its harsh highlands and ancient ruins, are best explored by camping there. Outdoor lovers may explore Mexico's natural beauty while reveling in the freedom and simplicity of camping thanks to the variety of alternatives offered.

The Baja California Peninsula is one of Mexico's most well-liked camping locations. White sand beaches, clean waterways, and chances for water sports like snorkeling, diving, and fishing are all features of Baja's spectacular coastal landscapes. Camping areas with beachside camping options include Bahia de los Angeles, Bahia Concepcion, and Cabo Pulmo National Park, where you may pitch your tent and experience spectacular ocean views.

The Yucatan Peninsula's Riviera Maya is another area where people like to camp. Beautiful cenotes, subterranean rivers, and Mayan ruins may all be found in this region. There are camping alternatives close to Tulum, where you may set up the tent in the forest and visit local cenotes or the ruins of Tulum. Some campgrounds provide facilities like restrooms, showers, and even access to power.

*Mexico travel guide 2023*

The Sierra Gorda area in Queretaro, central Mexico, provides breathtaking natural scenery and camping options. A UNESCO World Heritage Site, the Sierra Gorda Biosphere Reserve is home to mountains, canyons, waterfalls, and unusual flora and animals. You may get close to nature, stroll beautiful routes, and swim in natural pools at campgrounds like Puente de Dios and Media Luna.

Camping is also an option close to Mexico City, and there are several possibilities in the neighborhood. Just outside the city, the Desierto de los Leones National Park has camping places surrounded by pine trees and mountain bike and hiking routes. Southwest of Mexico City, atop a volcanic summit called Nevado de Toluca National Park, camping is possible with breathtaking views of the mountains and crater lake.

- It's crucial to have the right camping gear, such as a tent, sleeping bags, cooking utensils, and other essentials, while going camping in Mexico. It's also a good idea to check local laws since certain places can have restrictions on camping and campfires, such as requiring licenses.

- Planning a camping trip also requires taking the weather and time of year into account. It's crucial to pack appropriately and be ready for variations in temperature and precipitation while traveling to Mexico since the country may experience a variety of weather conditions.

Camping in Mexico is a wonderful way to discover the country's varied landscapes, get closer to nature, and engage in outdoor sports. Mexico's camping alternatives provide an exciting and engaging way to experience the nation's natural marvels, whether you choose seaside camping, jungle excursions, or mountain getaways.

# CHAPTER SEVEN

## Budget Friendly Restaurants In Mexico

Mexican food is well-known for being savory and delicious, and it can be found in a wide range of eateries, from high-end institutions to street sellers. There are many possibilities for inexpensive eateries that provide genuine and great meals for individuals who are traveling on a tight budget.

- The taqueria is a well-liked low-cost eating choice. Taquerias, which may be found all across Mexico, provide a variety of tacos, burritos, and other native cuisine. These casual, tiny eateries provide reasonably priced, tasty cuisine. In Mexico City, two well-known taquerias are El Califa and El Farolito.

- The mercado, or neighborhood market, is another place to get affordable food.

Mercados are often crowded, vibrant locations where sellers provide fresh foods including meats and veggies. You may try delectable Mexican cuisine at reasonable costs at several of the mercados' little eateries or food stands. The Mercado San Juan in Mexico City, for instance, offers a vast range of cuisine selections from all around Mexico.

- Several inexpensive eateries provide vegetarian and vegan alternatives for folks who have these dietary restrictions. The well-known vegetarian business Por Siempre Vegano provides a variety of plant-based meals in Mexico City at reasonable costs.

- The last fantastic choice for inexpensive eating in Mexico is street food. All around the nation, you may find street vendors selling anything from elotes (corn on the cob) and churros to tacos and tamales. Although the quality and hygiene of street food might vary greatly, it's often the finest way to taste real Mexican tastes and cuisine.

Overall, Mexico has a wide variety of inexpensive eating establishments. There is food to suit every taste and price range, whether you want traditional Mexican fare or cuisines from across the world.

# Mid-range Restaurants In Mexico

For those looking for a mid-range eating experience, Mexico provides a broad variety of restaurants that strike a compromise between quality and price. The nation is recognized for its bustling culinary scene. These budget-friendly restaurants provide a tasty and fulfilling eating experience without breaking the bank, serving anything from traditional Mexican food to cuisines from across the world.

- There are several mid-range restaurants in Mexico City, the nation's capital and culinary center, that offer dishes from all across the country. Popular options include La Casa de Tono, which specializes on classic Mexican cuisine including pozole, enchiladas, and chiles en nogada. Another well-known eatery, El Cardenal, is renowned for serving up traditional Mexican breakfast and brunch dishes like chilaquiles and molletes.

- Mexico City has a variety of mid-range alternatives for individuals who want to experience different foreign tastes. Pujol, run by famous chef Enrique Olvera, presents a contemporary take on Mexican food with dishes that combine customary ingredients and preparation methods with fresh plating. Maximo Bistrot, a French-inspired eatery renowned for its seasonal cuisine and focus on local, organic products, is another noteworthy choice.

- Fresh seafood and foreign cuisine are readily available in mid-range restaurants in coastal cities like Cancun and Playa del Carmen. La Habichuela is a well-liked option in Cancun that offers authentic Yucatecan food in a picturesque setting. Alux is a special restaurant in Playa del Carmen that serves a blend of Mexican and foreign cuisines inside a natural cave.

- Numerous choices for mid-range eating are also available in other cities including Guadalajara and Oaxaca. Santo Coyote is a well-known restaurant in Guadalajara that serves authentic Jalisco cuisine, including delectable birria and tequila-based beverages. The restaurant Casa Oaxaca in Oaxaca combines local specialties with global influences to create an unforgettable dining experience.

- It's important to note that mid-range restaurants in Mexico often emphasize using fresh, locally produced ingredients to create dishes that highlight the rich culinary traditions of the nation. Additionally, a lot of mid-range eateries have prix-fixe menus or lunch specials, which further reduces the price.

- Consider visiting the area where you'll be eating and asking locals or reliable travel sites for advice to make the most of your experience at midrange restaurants in Mexico. By doing this, you may find undiscovered treasures and family-run restaurants that have genuine tastes and a welcoming atmosphere.

Overall, Mexico's mid-range eateries provide a wonderful chance to enjoy delectable food without spending a lot of money. With a variety of alternatives available, you may savor traditional Mexican fare, discover other cuisines, and take in Mexico's thriving culinary scene while keeping your expenses in check.

## Luxury Restaurants In Mexico

Mexico is a nation renowned for its extensive culinary history, and it is home to many opulent restaurants that provide exceptional dining experiences. These high-end restaurants provide a genuinely opulent dining experience by combining superb cuisine, flawless service, and gorgeous décor.

- Several upscale eateries in Mexico City, the nation's capital and culinary powerhouse, have won recognition on a global scale. Pujol is a fine dining institution that honors Mexican ingredients and culinary traditions and is run by famous chef Enrique Olvera. Innovative dishes that highlight the variety of Mexican cuisine are included on the tasting menu. Another noteworthy restaurant is Quintonil, where Chef Jorge Vallejo crafts elegant and creative dishes by fusing traditional Mexican ingredients with cutting-edge cooking methods.

- Another place with a posh eating scene is San Miguel de Allende. Enrique Olvera, a renowned chef, is in charge of Moxi, a restaurant within the Hotel Matilda. The eatery provides modern Mexican cuisine with meals that are flavorful and use fresh local ingredients. A fantastic eating experience may be had in the chic and elegant environment provided by the ambiance.

- There are upscale eateries in coastal areas like Los Cabos and Riviera Maya that make the most of their breathtaking locations. Flora's Field Kitchen in Los Cabos is located on a farm and provides a farm-to-table dining experience with a focus on organic and regional foods. There is a calm and lovely ambiance created by the restaurant's outside seating, which looks out into the magnificent surroundings. Aldea Corazon, a beautiful eatery in Riviera Maya with a menu that emphasizes traditional Mexican food with a modern touch, is nestled in a verdant garden.

- Additionally, upscale eateries that provide a blend of world tastes are often found in luxury resorts in seaside towns. For instance, the Nizuc Resort & Spa in Cancun has some luxury eating establishments, such as Ramona, which serves a classy menu influenced by

Mexican and Mayan cuisine. The restaurant has a classy atmosphere and stunning coastal views.

- Be ready to pay more while eating at upscale establishments in Mexico. These establishments pride themselves on their immaculate presentation and superior service. It is strongly advised to make reservations, particularly during busy times or at special events. It's a good idea to confirm the restaurant's standards in advance since there can be dress regulations in place.

The fine dining establishments in Mexico provide a gastronomic experience that highlights the nation's unique tastes and culinary inventiveness. These restaurants provide an incredible voyage through the world of food, where originality, elegance, and outstanding tastes meet to produce a veritable feast for the senses, from the sophisticated avenues of Mexico City to the gorgeous coasts.

# Cafes And Coffee Shops In Mexico

Mexico is a nation that values its coffee culture and has a beautiful selection of cafes and coffee shops that serve all types of coffee lovers. These locations provide a refuge for coffee enthusiasts to indulge in their enthusiasm for the rich, fragrant beverage, from busy metropolitan centers to peaceful historical settlements.

- Mexican cafés have a welcoming ambiance that often reflects the colorful cultural history of the nation. You can find the perfect coffee shop in Mexico, whether you're looking for a quiet nook to read a book, a place to meet up with friends, or a place to people-watch.

- The classic "cafeteria" is one kind of coffee shop that is quite common in Mexico. These businesses provide a variety of coffee alternatives, ranging from the traditional café Americano to decadent espresso-based drinks. A selection of baked foods and pastries are often available at cafeterias, which are ideal for combining with your preferred cup of coffee. Numerous of these locations also have a variety of light breakfast and lunch choices, making them an excellent place to start your day or stop for a break while exploring.

- Mexico is home to an increasing number of specialty coffee shops for those looking for a more artisanal and distinctive coffee experience. These businesses concentrate on locating premium beans from various parts of Mexico and the rest of the globe. They place a high value on the art of producing coffee, using trained baristas to make each cup with care and accuracy. Here, you may sample different taste profiles, test out various brewing techniques, and discover where the beans come from.

- Along with the coffee itself, these specialized coffee shops often have a fashionable and modern atmosphere with sustainable practices and simple design. Additionally, many of these places work closely with neighborhood growers to promote fair trade principles and the local coffee-growing communities.

- Also embracing the idea of "terrazas," or outside dining spaces, are Mexican coffee businesses. Customers may sip their coffee on these patios while taking in the lively ambiance of their surroundings. The outside sitting choices enhance the coffee shop experience by adding a layer of appeal, whether it's in a busy city center, a charming cobblestone street, or a gorgeous courtyard.

- Cafes and coffee shops are an essential component of Mexico's cultural landscape, from the hip sections of Mexico City to the quaint colonial settlements of Oaxaca and San Miguel de Allende. They act as gathering places for conversation, sources of art inspiration, and places to unwind in addition to being places to have a wonderful cup of coffee.

So, Mexico's cafes and coffee shops have plenty to offer, whether you're a connoisseur hunting for the ideal espresso shot or just looking for a quiet place to rest. Enjoy the tastes, appreciate the aromas, and immerse yourself in the vibrant coffee culture that permeates this fascinating nation.

# CHAPTER EIGHT

## Spanish Cuisines To Try

Spanish food is recognized for its complex tastes, high-quality ingredients, and wide geographical variation. Spain has a rich culinary heritage that has been inspired by many different nations, and it has a broad variety of delectable foods that are worth tasting. Here are some delectable Spanish dishes:

- Paella: A tasty rice meal made with a mix of meat, seafood, and vegetables, paella is a Valencian specialty. It is a mainstay of Spanish cooking and is available in many versions, including Valencian paella, which includes rabbit and chicken, and seafood paella, which includes shrimp, mussels, and clams.

- Tapas are appetizers or tiny servings that are designed to be shared. They are available in a broad range of dishes, such as gambas al ajillo (garlic shrimp), albondigas (meatballs in tomato sauce), and patatas bravas (fried potatoes with spicy tomato sauce). It's a terrific way to enjoy a variety of Spanish cuisines and to sample a variety of tapas.

- Jamón Ibérico is a specialty of Spain produced from cured ham from Iberian pigs reared on acorns. The ham is matured for a long time, giving it a taste that is rich and potent. It is often served thinly sliced and eaten with bread or cheese or on its own.

- Gazpacho is a cool soup that is produced by blending tomatoes, bell peppers, cucumbers, garlic, and olive oil. It demonstrates the use of fresh ingredients in Spanish cuisine and is ideal for hot summer days.

- Pisto: A vegetable stew cooked with tomatoes, onions, peppers, and zucchini that is similar to ratatouille. It is a common meal in Spanish homes and is often served with eggs as a side dish or as a main entrée.

- Churros are a popular delicacy in Spain; they are deep-fried pastries made of dough. Usually, a cup of rich hot chocolate is included with them for dipping. Churros are a delicious delight that shouldn't be missed since they are soft on the inside and crisp on the exterior.

- Spanish omelet, or tortilla Espanola, is a traditional meal that combines eggs, potatoes, and onions. It's a common ingredient in Spanish cooking and is great as a tapa, in a sandwich, or as a major dish.

These are just a handful of mouthwatering Spanish dishes to sample. Spain's cuisine will fulfill the needs of every food lover, from substantial stews to tasty tapas. So, savor Spain's many tastes and culinary customs and acquaint yourself with its thriving culinary legacy.

# International Cuisines To Try

Mexico offers a unique tapestry of tastes that reflect its varied cultural background and foreign influences, making it a gourmet haven. Even while Mexican food is well-known globally, the whole nation offers a vast variety of other cuisines, making it a melting pot of tastes from across the globe. We'll look at some of the foreign foods you really must sample whilst in Mexico in this section.

- Italian food: Mexican cuisine has embraced the culinary traditions of Italy. You may enjoy genuine Italian food with a Mexican flair everywhere from classic trattorias to hip pizzerias. Enjoy al dente pasta dishes, creamy risottos, and wood-fired pizzas topped with regional ingredients. For a dining experience that will live long in the memory, don't forget to complement your meal with quality Italian wine.

- Mediterranean cuisine: Mexico has benefited from the tastes of the Mediterranean. A delicious variety of foods influenced by the coastal cuisines of Greece, Spain, and Morocco are served at Mediterranean restaurants. Enjoy succulent kebabs, delicious tagines, fresh seafood, and colorful salads with olive oil drizzles. Your taste senses will be transported by the distinctive flavor fusion created by the mix of Mediterranean ingredients with Mexican influences.

- Japanese cuisine has been more popular around the globe, and Mexico is no exception. Major cities are home to teppanyaki grills, ramen restaurants, and sushi bars that provide a flavor of Japan in the middle of Mexico. Enjoy a steamy bowl of ramen, indulge in some sushi rolls, and watch as talented chefs cook your food right in front of you. A great culinary treat is a Mexican food with a Japanese influence.

- Middle Eastern Food: Lebanese and Turkish restaurants are getting more and more well-liked in Mexico, where Middle Eastern food has found a warm home. Enjoy delectable kebabs, tasty falafel, savory hummus, and fresh tabbouleh. You'll be taken to the busy streets of Beirut or Istanbul thanks to the flavorful spice blend and conventional cooking methods.

- Asian Fusion Cuisine: Asian fusion restaurants are becoming a common sight in Mexico's dining scene as globalization continues to influence gastronomic trends. These restaurants provide a unique fusion of Mexican ingredients and cooking methods with Asian tastes. Try Asian-inspired tacos that harmoniously combine soy and chili sauces, savor fusion sushi rolls that explode with flavor, and discover creative recipes that combine the best of both cultures.

- American food: There are many different American cuisine alternatives available in Mexico. You can get scrumptious barbeque, succulent steaks grilled to perfection, and juicy burgers everywhere from typical American restaurants to luxury steakhouses. Enjoy substantial sandwiches, buffalo wings, and other comfort food favorites like macaroni and cheese. Your gastronomic tour of Mexico is made more comfortable by American food.

- French food is a must-try in Mexico if you're looking for sophisticated tastes and exquisite dining experiences. Exquisite meals that highlight the beauty of French culinary skills are served at French restaurants. French food in Mexico mixes French sartorial refinement with regional flare, from delicate pastries and buttery croissants to rich sauces and expertly prepared meats.

These are just a few examples of the many different cuisines you may enjoy in Mexico.

You may satiate your appetites with a variety of gastronomic delicacies, whether you're in the mood for anything from Italy, Japan, or the Mediterranean. While experiencing the dynamic essence of Mexico, embrace the combination of tastes, discover new gastronomic frontiers, and allow your taste senses to go on an incredible voyage throughout the globe.

# CHAPTER NINE

## 10 - Days Itinerary To Explore Mexico

Mexico is a nation rich in history, culture, and scenic beauty. There is something for everyone in this varied nation, from the historic Mayan ruins to the lively street art of Mexico City. Here is a fantastic 10-day travel schedule for Mexico.

**Day 1-2: Mexico City**

Start your journey in Mexico City, a vibrant city. Start by strolling around the Zocalo, the city's historic core. The National Palace, the magnificent Metropolitan Cathedral, and the Templo Mayor ruins may all be found here. After that, go to Coyoacan, a hipster district, to see the Frida Kahlo Museum and sample some of the city's greatest cuisine at the Mercado de Coyoacan.

## Day 3 - 4: Oaxaca

Take a flight from Mexico City to Oaxaca, a city in the same-named state's southern region. Oaxaca is renowned for its vibrant marketplaces, mouth watering food, and vibrant indigenous culture. Spend your days discovering the historic buildings of the city, admiring the magnificent Santo Domingo Church, and purchasing trinkets in the Benito Juarez Market. Enjoy live music and dancing performances in the evenings in the central plaza.

## Day 5 - 6: Hierve el Agua and Monte Alban

Take a day excursion to the historic remains of Monte Alban, which are close to the city of Oaxaca. This pre-Columbian location, which formerly served as the Zapotec civilization's capital, has stunning views of the valleys around. After seeing the ruins, visit Hierve el Agua, a natural marvel where you can relax in mineral springs and take in the breathtaking petrified waterfalls.

## Day 7-8: San Cristóbal de las Casas

Fly to Tuxtla Gutierrez, then enjoy a beautiful drive to San Cristobal de las Casas, a magnificent historical town in the state of Chiapas. Spend your days strolling around the town's vibrant streets, admiring the stunning cathedrals, and perusing the markets. The adjacent Sumidero Canyon is a must-visit day excursion where you can go on a boat tour and see crocodiles, monkeys, and many bird species.

## Day 9-10: Tulum

Tulum, a seaside town on the Caribbean Sea, is a great place to unwind and spend time on the beach. Visit the Tulum Mayan ruins, which are next to the beach, and take advantage of the crystal-clear seas for swimming and snorkeling. Dine at some of the town's top seafood establishments in the evenings and take in the laid-back beach ambiance.

With this schedule, you may explore some of Mexico's most famous sites in only 10 days while also experiencing a wonderful combination of culture, history, and natural beauty. Don't be afraid to prolong your vacation or change this schedule to fit your interests and tastes since there is much more to see in this large and varied nation.

# CONCLUSION

We hope that we have succeeded in conveying the genuine spirit and attraction of this amazing nation as we come to a close with our travel guide to Mexico. Mexico is a magical country with a colorful tapestry of fascinating culture, stunning scenery, and kind people. It is a location that welcomes a variety of tourists, from thrill-seekers to history buffs, beach lovers to foodies. Mexico is a hidden gem just waiting to be discovered with its wide variety of attractions and limitless opportunities.

Each area has something special to offer, from the crowded streets of Mexico City to the serene beaches of the Yucatan Peninsula. The impressive accomplishments of ancient civilizations are shown in the ruins of Chichen Itza and Teotihuacan, which transport us back to antiquity. The country's magnificent architecture and cultural legacy are on display in the historic towns of Guanajuato, Oaxaca, and San Miguel de Allende.

Mexico's natural splendors are breathtaking. The lush forests of Chiapas and the Copper Canyon entice us to set out on daring excursions, while the crystal-clear waters of the cenotes beg us to plunge into their enigmatic depths. The gorgeous beaches of Cancun, Tulum, and Playa del Carmen provide chances for water sports and leisure in the sun.

The tastes and traditions of Mexico are celebrated in Mexican cuisine. Every food has a tale to tell, from the zesty joys of street tacos to the deep mole sauces and cool aguas frescas. A gastronomic experience unlike any other may be had by perusing the neighborhood markets and enjoying the regional delicacies. Not to mention the world-famous tequila and mezcal, which give every gathering an additional dash of festivity.

Beyond its views and smells, Mexico stands out for its people's friendliness and kindness. Mexicans are well known for being hospitable, having a positive outlook on life, and being eager to share their traditions and customs with others. You'll experience a true connection that will stick with you long after your trip is over, whether you're taking part in a vibrant fiesta, learning the routines of traditional dances, or conversing with locals in earnest.

While there are many options for discovery and adventure in Mexico, it is important to travel ethically and with consideration for the local people and the surrounding areas. Be respectful of the local traditions, pick up a few basic Spanish words, and be aware of how your behavior may affect the locations you visit. We can guarantee that future generations will continue to appreciate Mexico's beauty and richness by vacationing responsibly.

We hope that our travel guide has given you insightful information, practical advice, and a feeling of anticipation as you get ready to start your Mexican experience. We hope you have a life-changing experience amid the breathtaking beauty and cultural diversity of Mexico.

So prepare your belongings, embrace the spirit of exploration, and let Mexico capture your heart. Discover its historical treasures, take in its breathtaking scenery, delight in its delicious food, and establish connections with its extraordinary people. Prepare to discover the mystique hidden inside the colorful tapestry of Mexico, a place that will make an enduring impression on your spirit. Have a safe trip, and may your time in Mexico be enriched by many magical moments and amazing experiences.

Printed in Great Britain
by Amazon

28030239R00076